Handwriting Without Tears®
by Learning Without Tears

Name: _____

Building Writers

Patrick scored. The crowd cheered!

Baseball helmets are very hard.

I think soccer is the best team sport.

LEARNING
Without Tears®

8001 MacArthur Blvd
Cabin John, MD 20818
LWTears.com | 888.983.8409

Authors: Jan Z. Olsen, OTR and Allison Anderson, M.A. Ed.
Curriculum Designers: Christina Bretz, MS, OTR/L and Tania Ferrandino, OTR/L
In-House Illustrators: Jan Z. Olsen, OTR, Julie Koborg, Aaron Jackson, Carol Johnston, and Sammie Simon
Graphic Designers: Carol Johnston and Julie Koborg
Editor: Kathryn Fox

Copyright © 2022 Learning Without Tears
Second Edition
ISBN: 978-1-952970-90-0
123456789PAH232221
Printed in the USA

The contents of this consumable workbook are protected by US copyright law. If a workbook has been purchased for a child, the author and Learning Without Tears give limited permission to copy pages for additional practice or homework for that child. No copied pages from this book can be given to another person without written permission from Learning Without Tears.

Get to Know BUILDING WRITERS
By Learning Without Tears

Workbook Design

This workbook is designed with both teachers and young writers in mind. The activities in this book provide age-appropriate and engaging writing practice. Each activity can be easily incorporated into a writing block as independent writing or as whole group practice to meet your students' varying needs.

In this book, students are provided carefully scaffolded opportunities to grow as independent writers. Each page has easily accessible and child-friendly resources to ensure writers at all stages are supported as they learn the building blocks of successful writing. Activities in this book are intuitive and engaging, with exercises specifically designed to provide students with a framework to develop core writing skills.

This book's developmentally designed content gradually prepares students for independent writing across the three main writing types: Narrative, Information, and Opinion/Argument. In each section, students are introduced to the key elements of each writing type in a purposefully organized sequence. Specifically chosen templates (familiar from previous activities) are at the end of each section for further practice. These templates can be adapted in order to apply the learned writing skills in each section to curriculum-specific content, student-chosen topics, or other individualized subjects.

Additional Resources

Teacher tips for using this workbook and additional resources are available online at **LWTears.com/BuildingWriters**.
For additional writing practice, use our Writing Journals.

Teacher Resource!

© 2022 Learning Without Tears

TABLE OF CONTENTS

You Are A Writer

You Are A Writer!.............................4–5

Narrative Writing

Narrative Writing Introduction............6–9

Travel To Egypt 10

I Can Draw Pyramids & Camels!........... 11

Sports & Feelings 12–13

Playing Sports 14

A Baseball Story................................ 15

The Three Little Pigs.....................16–17

What's Hatching?.........................18–19

The Little Red Hen.......................20–23

Short Stories 24–25

New Girl 26

I Can Draw Feelings!.......................... 27

The Turtle & The Rabbit 28

Feeling Proud 29

Writing Templates 30–33

TABLE OF CONTENTS

Information Writing

Information Writing Introduction 34–37
Sports Gear 38–39
Amazing Animals 40–41
Baby Animals 42–43
Jesse Owens 44
Running A Race 45
Animal Coverings 46–47
Draw Like Marc Chagall! 48
Marc Chagall 49
Self-Portrait: Frida Kahlo 50
Frida Kahlo 51
Animal Helpers 52–53
Field Day 54
Wacky Sports 55
Draw Like Andy Warhol! 56
Andy Warhol 57
Animal Eggs 58–59
Tortoise & Turtle 60
I Can Draw Turtles! 61
Studying Animals 62–63
Writing Templates 64–67

Opinion/Argument Writing

Opinion/Argument Writing Introduction 68–71
Sports Players 72
Games 73
Yoga 74–75
Scary Animals: Shark or Bear? 76
Feeling Scared 77
Salty & Sweet 78
Farm Animals 79
Pick A Player 80
Sports Safety 81
Studying Animals 82–83
Favorite Superpower 84
Writing Templates 85–86

YOU ARE A WRITER!

 Writers write about subjects.
Copy the sentences or write your own.

Writers tell what subjects do.

Some elephants work.

Writers describe things.

Elephant trunks are hollow.

Writers tell what things are.

Elephants are mammals.

YOU ARE A WRITER!

 Copy the sentences or write your own.

Writers ask questions with question words.
Who? What? Where? When? Why? How?

What is a trunk?

Writers ask questions without question words.

Do elephants eat plants?

Writers show excitement.

I won!

Writers give commands.

Don't look.

Building (Narrative) Writers

Patrick scored. The crowd cheered!

NARRATIVE WRITING

✏️ Narrative writing tells a story in order. Read the story.

Beginning:
It was time for Ellie's big day.

Middle:

The elephant painter came.

End:

When he finished, Ellie looked bright and beautiful!

Narrative Writing Checklist

☑ I wrote a story in order.

☑ I wrote details.

☑ I wrote an ending.

NARRATIVE WRITING
✏️ Copy the story.

Ellie looks for a drink.

Ellie finds a little pool.

NARRATIVE WRITING

✏️ Copy the story. Draw what happens at the end.

She drinks and splashes in

the water.

TRAVEL TO EGYPT

✏️ Write what you can see, ride, and taste in Egypt.

- see
- ride
- taste

pyramids

camels

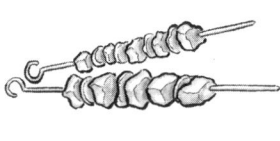
kebabs

Egypt

I can

I CAN DRAW PYRAMIDS & CAMELS!

✏️ Draw a pyramid and a camel.

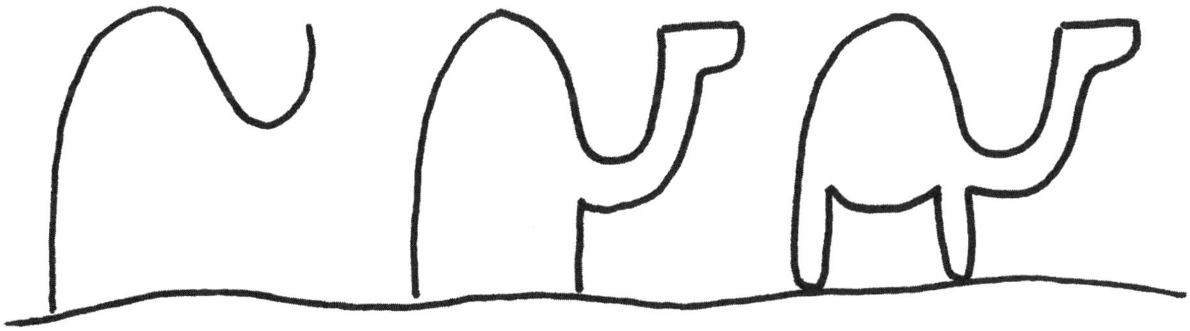

SPORTS & FEELINGS

✎ Write what happened and how each person feels.

- scored
- goal
- excited

Jim scored a

He feels

- lost
- race
- upset

Allie

She

SPORTS & FEELINGS

 Write what happened and how each person feels.

- won
- trophy
- proud

Meg

She

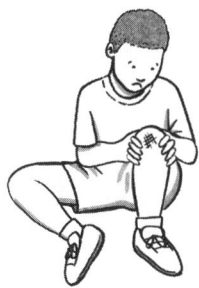

- hurt
- knee
- worried

Malik

He

PLAYING SPORTS

✏️ Write what you can do in each sport.

- kick
- soccer ball

Soccer is a sport.

I can _____ a soccer ball.

- hit
- baseball

Baseball

- shoot
- basketball

Basketball

A BASEBALL STORY

✏️ Tell the baseball story.

- hit baseball

- ran bases

- scored and won

It was Dave's turn to bat.

THE THREE LITTLE PIGS

Tell the story of the three little pigs and the big, bad wolf.

three little pigs

houses

straw sticks bricks

The three little pigs built

big, bad wolf

house of straw

The

THE THREE LITTLE PIGS

✏️ Tell the story of the three little pigs and the big, bad wolf.

big, bad wolf

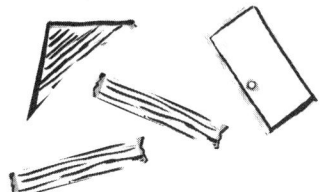
house of sticks

The _____

run!

house of bricks
all safe!

They _____

WHAT'S HATCHING?

 Write a story about what hatches.

- egg
- cracks a little

First,

- egg
- cracks more

Next,

- baby alligator
- hatches

Last,

WHAT'S HATCHING?

✏️ Draw an animal hatching. Write a story about an animal that hatches.

THE LITTLE RED HEN

✏ Use the information below to complete the story about The Little Red Hen.

 - plant the wheat

Who will help plant the wheat?

- cut the wheat

Who will help

- to the mill

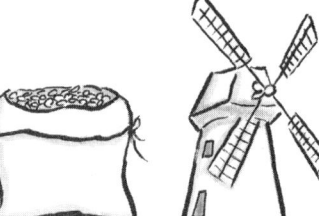

Who will take it

20 Building Writers B: *Narrative Writing* © 2022 Learning Without Tears

THE LITTLE RED HEN

✏️ Use the information below to complete the story about The Little Red Hen.

 - mix the dough

Who will help

 - bake the bread

Who will help

  - eat the bread

Who will help

THE LITTLE RED HEN

 Answer the questions with complete sentences.

Who will help me?

Who asked for help?
Hen

Not I!

Was Dog helpful?

Not I!

Was Duck helpful?

THE LITTLE RED HEN

 Answer the question with complete sentences.

Not I!

Was Cat helpful?

No bread for you!

Did the Little Red Hen share?

Would you share?

I

SHORT STORIES

✏️ Read the short story. Then, write your own story. Write new characters (who), a new setting (where), and a new plot (why).

Jack and Jill

went up the hill

to fetch

a pail of water.

Who? ⟶ _____

Where? ⟶ went _____

Why? ⟶ to _____

SHORT STORIES

✏️ Read the short story. Then, write your own story. Write new characters (who), a new setting (where), and a new plot (why).

Old Mother Hubbard went to the cupboard to get her poor dog a bone.

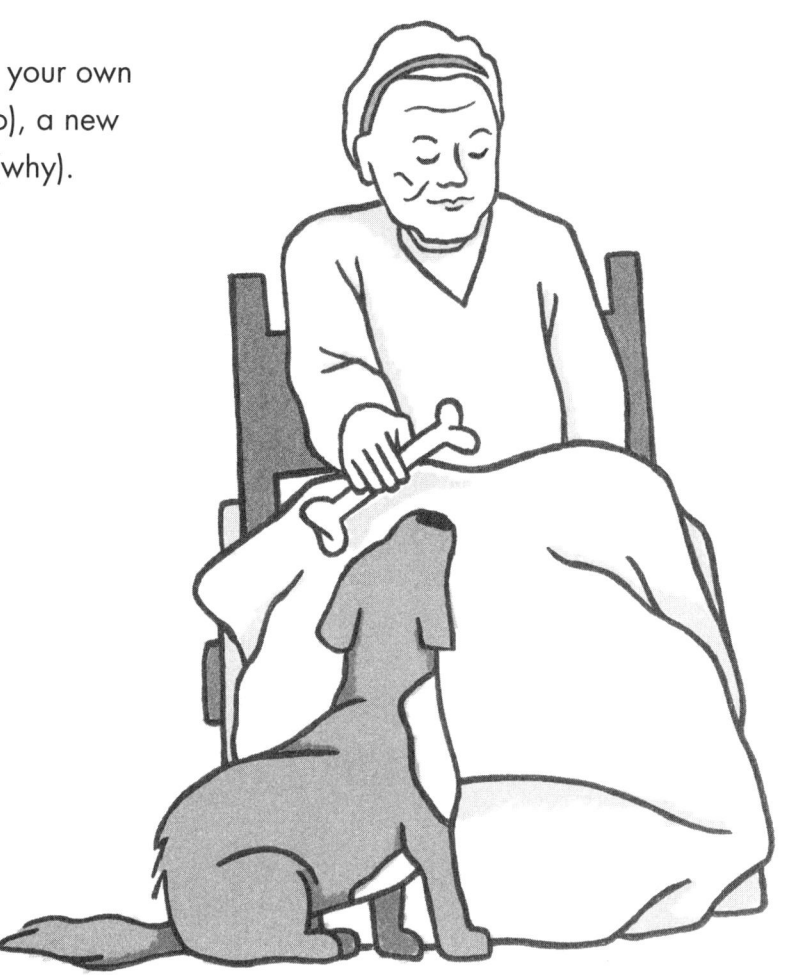

Who? ⟶ _____

Where? ⟶ went _____

Why? ⟶ to _____

© 2022 Learning Without Tears   Building Writers B: **Narrative Writing**   **25**

NEW GIRL

✏️ Use the illustrations and information below to complete the story about a new girl at school.

- alone at lunch
- sad

Sue was alone at lunch.

She felt _____

- beside Sue
- friendly

Kim sat _____

Kim was _____

- became friends
- had a great lunch

Sue and Kim _____

They _____

26 *Building Writers B: Narrative Writing*

I CAN DRAW FEELINGS!

✏️ Draw a sad and a happy face. Write what makes you sad. Write what makes you happy.

sad

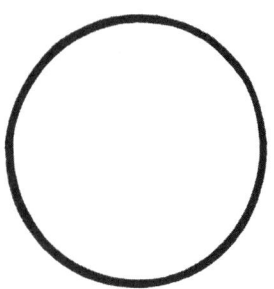

happy

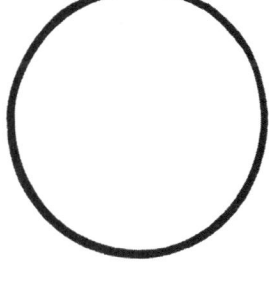

THE TURTLE & THE RABBIT

✎ Complete the story of the Turtle and the Rabbit using the information below.

Turtle, slow
Rabbit, fast

Rabbit made fun of Turtle for being slow. Turtle said, "Let's race!"

Turtle, ahead
Rabbit, rest

Turtle, won
Rabbit, lost

Turtle felt very proud!

FEELING PROUD

✏️ Draw and write about a time you felt proud.

TITLE/TOPIC: _____

First, _____

Next, _____

Last, _____

TITLE/TOPIC: _____

TITLE/TOPIC: _____

TITLE/TOPIC:

Building Information Writers

INFORMATION WRITING

✏️ Information writing tells facts. Read the example below.

Introduction:

Elephants are plant eaters.

Facts:

They eat grass and bushes.

Tree bark is their favorite food.

Conclusion:

Elephants eat a lot each day.

Information Writing Checklist

☑ I wrote a beginning sentence.

☑ I wrote facts about my topic.

☑ I wrote an ending sentence.

INFORMATION WRITING

✎ Label the parts of the elephant.

- ear
- trunk
- tusk
- tail

INFORMATION WRITING

✎ Copy the sentences about elephants. Use the previous page to write a new fact about another elephant body part.

Introduction:

Elephants are large animals.

Fact:

They have long trunks.

New Fact:

They have

Conclusion:

Elephants are gigantic!

SPORTS GEAR

✏️ Use the labels to write how sport players stay safe.

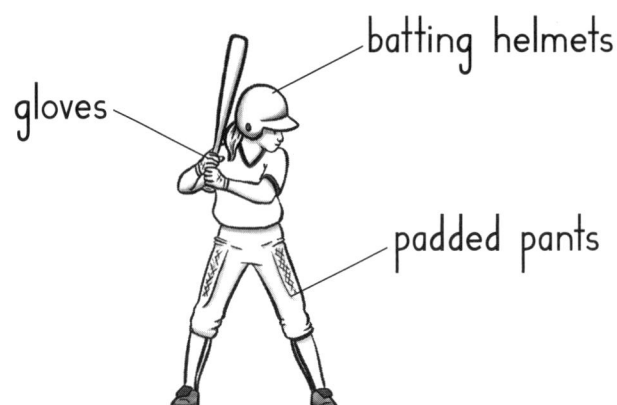

Softball players wear

Swimmers

SPORTS GEAR

✏️ Use the labels to write how sport players stay safe.

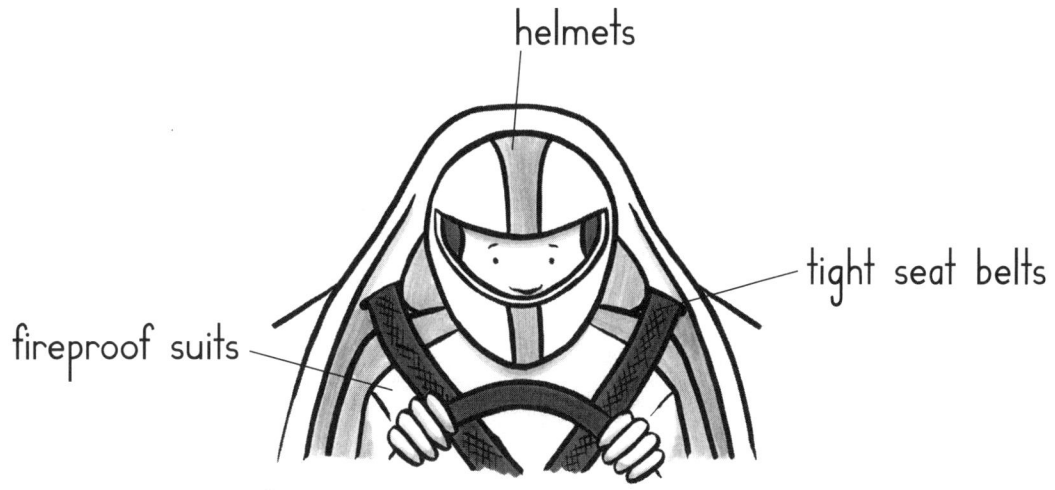

Race car drivers

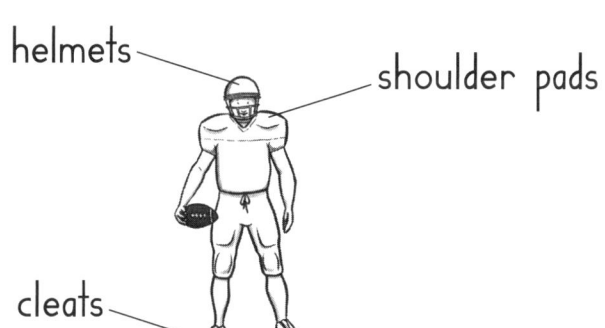

Football players

AMAZING ANIMALS

✏️ Write facts about each animal using the information below.

- has a long spiral tusk
- lives in icy Arctic water
- nicknamed unicorn of the sea

narwhal

A narwhal

salmon

- migrates to lay eggs
- is a blue, red, or silver color
- has gills

A salmon

AMAZING ANIMALS

✏️ Write facts about each animal using the information below.

cheetah

- is the fastest animal on land
- has special feet for running
- has spotted fur

A cheetah

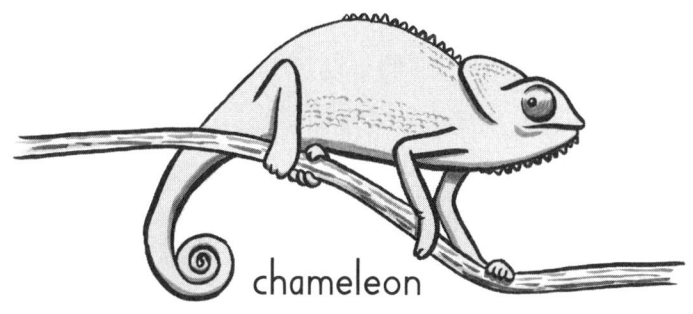
chameleon

- changes skin color
- sheds skin
- has sticky feet

A chameleon

BABY ANIMALS

✎ Write about what each animal is called as a baby and what they are called after they grow.

piglet   hairy hog

A baby pig is a
A piglet will grow up to be a

froglet   happy hopper

A baby frog

BABY ANIMALS

✎ Write about what each animal is called as a baby and what they are called after they grow.

an owlet

feathered flier

an eaglet

hardy hunter

JESSE OWENS

✎ Use the information on the page to write facts about the athlete Jesse Owens.

Jesse Owens

- famous African American athlete
- fast runner
- four gold medals
- 1936 Olympics
- world record-breaker

Jesse Owens

RUNNING A RACE

✏️ Write the steps to run a race.

- crouches low
- begin the race

The runner crouches low to begin the race.

- leans
- pulls up

- swings arms
- pumps legs

ANIMAL COVERINGS

 Write about the animal coverings.

panda
- fur
- thick

Some animals have fur.

A panda has thick fur.

snake
- scales
- dry

Some animals

A snake

peacock
- feathers
- colorful

ANIMAL COVERINGS

✎ Write about the animal coverings.

seal
- skin
- smooth

turtle
- shell
- hard

person
- skin
- _____

A person
I have

DRAW LIKE MARC CHAGALL!

✏️ Read the poem. Follow the steps to draw a horse.

Horses

Chagall painted red horses,

Green horses too.

I can draw horses and

Color them too.

MARC CHAGALL

✎ Write about the artist Marc Chagall.

Marc Chagall, painter

red and green horses

colorful people

Paris Opera House ceiling

Marc Chagall

SELF-PORTRAIT: FRIDA KAHLO

Color Frida Kahlo's self-portrait.

Frida painted 55 self-portraits.

FRIDA KAHLO

✏️ Write about the artist Frida Kahlo.

self-portrait

flowers and colorful clothes

husband, Diego Rivera

Frida Kahlo painted

She wore

She painted herself with

ANIMAL HELPERS

✏️ Write how dogs help humans using the facts below.

- guide people who can't see
- find lost people
- have a strong sense of smell
- can be police dogs

Dogs help humans.

_____
_____
_____
_____
_____

Dogs are great helpers.

ANIMAL HELPERS

✏️ Write how horses help humans.

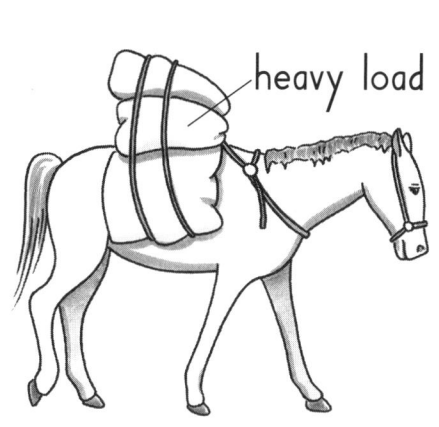

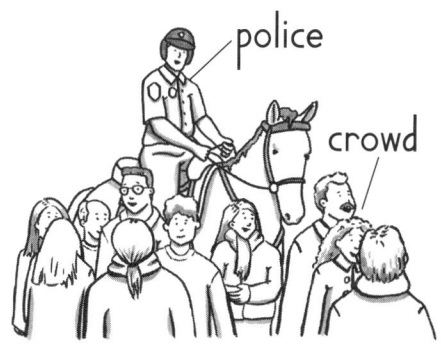

Horses help humans.

FIELD DAY

✏️ Write about field day games.

hula hoop

water balloon toss

tug of war

sack race

wheelbarrow race

We can play many games on field day.

Field day is fun!

WACKY SPORTS

✏️ Write about the wacky sports.

Camel racing is a sport.
Jockeys ride camels on a track.

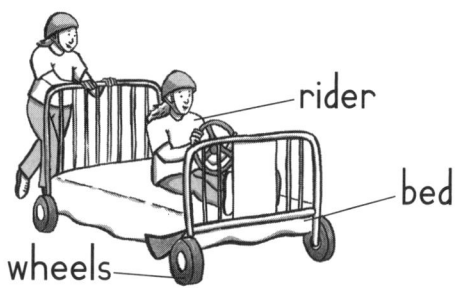

Bed racing

Cheese rolling

DRAW LIKE ANDY WARHOL!

✏️ Read the poem and information about Andy Warhol. Draw soup cans and cats.

32 Soup Cans

Andy painted one can,

And then many more.

He painted Campbell's soups,

All the soups in the store.

Andy Warhol lived with his mother and many, many cats.

ANDY WARHOL

✏️ Write about the artist Andy Warhol.

pop artist

mom

cats

soup can paintings

Andy Warhol was famous. He lived with

ANIMAL EGGS

✎ Use the information below to write facts about animals that lay eggs.

frogs

- many tiny eggs
- in water

ducks

- eggs with thick shells
- in nest in tall grass

lizards

- soft eggs
- in nest in dirt

ANIMAL EGGS

✎ Use the information below to write facts about animals that lay eggs.

fish	birds	butterflies
- soft	- hard	- round
- small	- shell	- tiny
- in water	- in nest	- on leaf

Animals lay different eggs.

TORTOISE & TURTLE

✎ Write about a tortoise and a turtle using the information below.

Tortoise

- lives on land
- can't swim
- feet for walking
- heavy shell

Turtle

- lives in or near water
- can swim
- flippers or webbed feet for swimming
- light shell

I CAN DRAW TURTLES!

✏️ Draw the missing parts. Color the turtles.

STUDYING ANIMALS

✎ Write how each person studies animals.

paleontologist

dig up

- dinosaurs
- plants
- fossils

Paleontologists _____

_____

_____

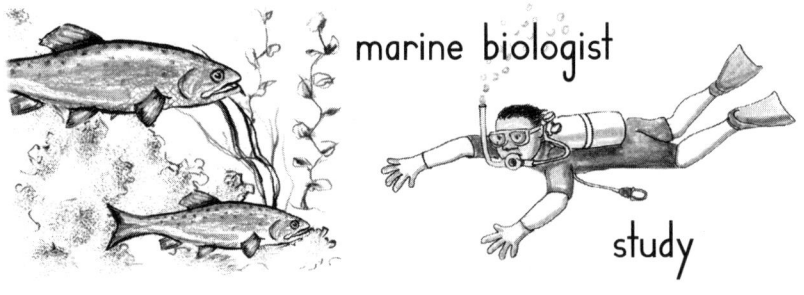

marine biologist

study

- fish
- dolphins
- whales

Marine biologists _____

_____

_____

STUDYING ANIMALS

✏️ Write how each person studies animals.

- elephants
- apes
- tigers

Zoologists _____

_____
_____

- insects
- ants
- spiders

Entomologists _____

_____
_____

TITLE/TOPIC: _____

TITLE/TOPIC:

TITLE/TOPIC: _____

TITLE/TOPIC:

Building Opinion/Argument Writers

I think soccer is the best team sport.

OPINION/ARGUMENT WRITING

✏️ Opinion/argument writing tells how you feel and gives reasons for your opinion/argument.

Introduction:

In my opinion/argument, elephants are more interesting than monkeys.

Reasons:

Elephants are more interesting because they sleep standing up.

I also like elephants because they are smart. They have great memories.

Conclusion:

Elephants are special animals.

Opinion/Argument Writing Checklist

☐ I wrote an introduction that tells my opinion/argument.

☐ I wrote reasons to support my opinion/argument.

☐ I wrote a conclusion.

OPINION/ARGUMENT WRITING

✎ Copy the opinion.

I do not think an elephant would be a good pet.

OPINION/ARGUMENT WRITING

✏️ Copy the sentences. Write a second reason why an elephant would not be a good pet.

Reason one:

Elephants need a lot of space.

Reason two:

Conclusion:

An elephant would not be a good pet for me!

SPORTS PLAYERS

✎ Write about what sports players do.

- ice skate
- pass pucks

Hockey players

- jump high
- serve tennis balls

Tennis players

GAMES

✏️ Write which game you would play and why.

Tic Tac Toe

- two players
- draw X or O
- three of the same in a row wins

Four in a Row

- two players
- line up red or black chips
- four of the same in a row wins

I would play _____

YOGA

✎ Write how you think the yoga pose got its name by looking at the pictures.

flamingo pose 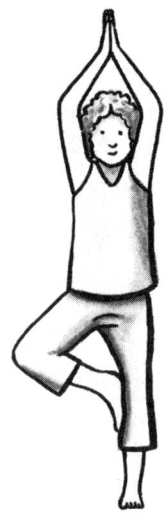   flamingo

This is named the flamingo pose because

YOGA

✏️ Write how you think the yoga pose got its name by looking at the pictures.

butterfly pose    butterfly

This is named the butterfly pose because

SCARY ANIMALS: SHARK OR BEAR?

✏️ Write which animal you think is scarier and explain why.

white shark

brown bear

- has sharp teeth
- can swim fast

- has sharp claws
- can climb quickly

I think the _____

is scarier because _____

FEELING SCARED

✏️ Draw and write about a time you felt scared.

I felt scared when

SALTY & SWEET

✏️ Write about which foods you like the best and why.

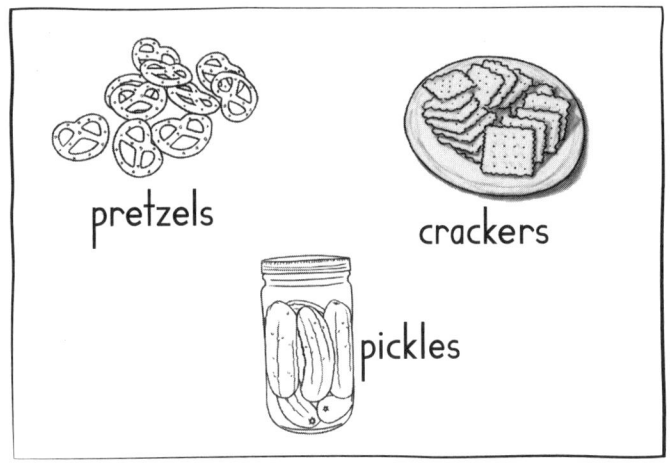

salty

sweet

FARM ANIMALS

✏️ You have a farm! Write which animals you would have and why. Use the information below to help write your opinion.

If I had a farm, I would have _____

sheep, wool

chickens, eggs

cows, milk

PICK A PLAYER

✎ Write about which sports player you would be and why. You can write about being a swimmer, basketball player, or any other sports player you choose.

swimmer   basketball player

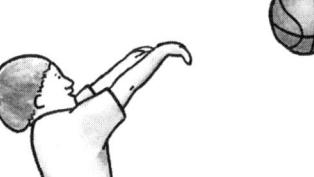

- swim laps
- pool
- race

- shoot baskets
- court
- team

I would be a _____

SPORTS SAFETY

✏️ Write how you can stay safe while playing sports.

water

healthy food

I can stay safe by drinking water and

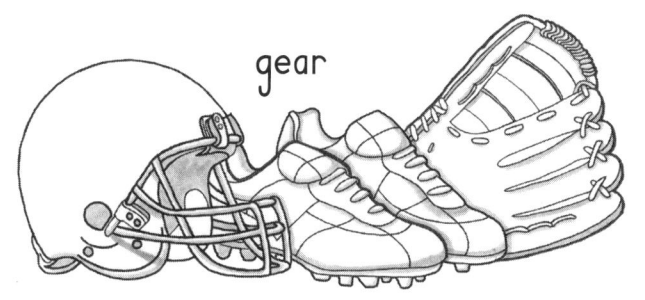

gear

follow rules

I

STUDYING ANIMALS

✎ Use the information below to write about Jane Goodall. Write what you think about her studies of chimpanzees.

Jane Goodall

chimpanzee

- anthropologist
- lived with chimps in Africa
- wrote books
- observed that chimps use tools and eat meat

STUDYING ANIMALS

✎ Pretend you want to be a scientist. Write which scientist you would like to be and why. You can choose from the options below or you can choose to be another type of scientist.

entomologist

- studies insects
- observes with microscope
- snails, bees, butterflies, and beetles

mammalogist

- studies mammals
- explores with binoculars
- bears, lions, pigs, and horses

I would like to be

FAVORITE SUPERPOWER

✏️ If you had a superpower, would you rather be able to fly, or turn invisible? Write your opinion and explain why.

I would rather

fly

turn invisible

TITLE/TOPIC: _____

I would rather

TITLE/TOPIC: _____

In my opinion,